Mug Cakes

Mug Cakes

40 SPEEDY CAKES TO MAKE IN A MICROWAVE

MIMA SINCLAIR

KYLE BOOKS

To my mum, who has never hidden her love of sugar,
and to my dad, who said I would grow out of mine.

First published in
Great Britain in 2014 by
Kyle Books, an imprint of
Kyle Cathie Ltd.
192–198 Vauxhall Bridge Road
London, SW1V 1DX
general.enquiries@kylebooks.com
www.kylebooks.com

10 9 8 7 6 5 4

ISBN 978 0 85783 267 2

Text © 2014 Mima Sinclair
Design © 2014 Kyle Books
Photographs © 2014 Tara Fisher

Mima Sinclair is hereby identified
as the author of this work in
accordance with Section 77 of
the Copyright, Designs and Patents
Act 1988.

Editor: Judith Hannam
Project editor: Vicki Murrell
Designer: Nicola Collings
Photographer: Tara Fisher
Food stylist: Mima Sinclair
Prop stylists: Wei Tang and Olivia
Wardle
Illustrations: Aaron Blecha
Production: Nic Jones and Gemma
John

A Cataloguing in Publication record
for this title is available from the
British Library.

Colour reproduction by ALTA
London
Printed and bound in Italy
by Printer Trento s.r.l.

CONTENTS

WHAT IS A MUG CAKE?

Make a cake in a mug, in a microwave, in less than 10 minutes, using simple ingredients you don't even have to weigh out, with no waste, no leftovers and little washing up? Where's the catch? There isn't one.

Conventional cake making can be tricky, as we've all learned through trial and error. There is such an exact science behind it that a bit too much of this, or not enough of that, can have dramatic consequences – both costly and time consuming. Mug cakes – instant cakes you make in the microwave using simple measures and minimal ingredients – on the other hand make baking so easy you will soon be creating your own recipes.

I experimented a lot with different approaches and quantities of ingredients, initially with mixed results. The main differences between an oven and a microwave are the way they heat food and the speed at which they do it. This effects two things – the microwave can't brown or crisp a cake and, just as it cooks the cake faster, it also drys it out faster if you overcook it. There were some explosions and a fair bit of mess, but as soon as I learnt a few do's and don'ts, I was creating perfect cakes time and time again. Once I'd mastered a deliciously light cake it was exciting seeing what flavours I could mix in and complement with fun icings and toppings. I'm a bit of a sugar addict, so for me it's all about the toppings! The possibilities are endless, and that's what is really exciting – not only can you make cake in the microwave, you can make cheesecakes, upside down pies, happy hour cocktails, cookies and more! They are perfect single-serving cakes to save you scoffing a whole baked one! They're also great for hungry kids, who'll think it's an extra treat to be able to make the cake themselves. And as dinner party desserts and unique party nibbles that will surely get people talking.

Mug cakes are fun quick fixes that you'll enjoy as soon as you decide you want one. The only problem is that when they are this easy every night becomes a mug cake night!

INTRODUCTION

THE
INGREDIENTS

BUTTER

In testing, I found that soft, room temperature butter was best for ensuring cakes have a delicious rich flavour, but you can also use a flavourless oil (such as sunflower or vegetable) or even margarine. Just swap in the recipe in place of the butter as the measurements are like for like. If you use butter straight from the fridge it will just take a little longer to melt.

EGGS

Always use medium eggs as other sizes will upset the balance of ingredients in the cake mix. I find they are best when used at room temperature, otherwise they can curdle easily and cause the mixture to separate. However, if this happens, it really is not a problem – the cake will just be a little less light.

SALT

This can be omitted if you wish, but using salt as a seasoning really enhances the overall flavour of both sweet and savoury cakes and intensifies them.

SUGAR

The recipes mainly call for caster or soft brown sugar as these have a finer texture than granulated and other coarser sugars, so are better for baking as they dissolve quicker when cooking. You can make your own caster sugar by briefly grinding granulated sugar in a food processor (although be careful you don't over-grind to a powder).

FLOUR

Self-raising flour is the most convenient to use as the balance of flour and baking powder has been measured out for you and saves you having to worry about over- or under-use of a raising agent. Nice and simple!

READY...
STEADY...

You need no special kitchen utensils or culinary baking skills – just a mug, a microwave and a few basic ingredients, so you're probably ready to go! However, as microwaves and explosions do occasionally go hand in hand, have a read of the below to avoid any mishaps and guarantee instant mug cake success.

THE MUG

Is it microwavable? This is important. If it isn't, the high heat of a microwave may cause it to crack and scald you. Check for a microwave symbol and if you can't see one perform the quick test on the right.

THE MICROWAVE

What type? Regrettably microwave ovens, like conventional ovens, do vary in power and age, which effects the cooking times so they are inevitably a little approximate. You may need to use your judgement to decide if it needs a little more or less cooking time. However, I have created these recipes using a standard microwave that will no doubt be very similar to what you have in your kitchen, and I always include three standard microwave power wattages so you have a few options. Use the closest to that of your microwave, follow the timings as a guideline and bear in mind the Essential Do's and Don'ts that follow and you will quickly get the hang of it.

THE MUG TEST

Place the (empty) mug in the microwave and heat for 1 minute. Take it out and feel its temperature. If it's lukewarm or cold then it should be fine, but if it's hot do not use it in your microwave.

Is it metal? Do not use metal mugs or anything with a metallic trim such as a gold band or pattern. They can produce dangerous sparks that could burn you or damage the microwave.

Size counts. The average size of a mug is 350ml. Check your favourite mug before you use it – if it is larger, it is not a problem, but if it is smaller you will need to leave a little of the mixture out to avoid a messy overflow. If you want to get inventive and start serving cakes in pots other than mugs, such as ramekins, jam jars, ice cream cones, cardboard cups, etc, then just bear in mind the size difference (they are often smaller) and don't over fill them. Or make two – one for you and a friend. Just remember to always avoid anything metal, even if it's just a tiny trimming.

Do not be disheartened if your cake sinks or explodes. The finished product will still taste delicious. You will soon work out the timings and quantities for your microwave.

Do not be tempted to keep cooking the cake until it browns or forms a crust – it never will! Unlike conventional ovens microwaves do not directly brown or caramelise food as they don't reach the necessary temperatures. If you continue to cook a mug cake it will just dry out.

THE ESSENTIAL
DO'S AND DON'TS

(OR HOW TO AVOID AN AWFUL MESS)

PREP

Do not over-whisk as this overaerates the cake batter and, once cooked you may discover air holes in the sponge (not ideal if your cake is in any kind of glass container).

Do not under-whisk either as this will also result in air pockets due to a mass of unmixed butter or flour. Whisk the ingredients together with a fork until the cake batter is smooth.

Do not overfill the mug. Two-thirds full is plenty as otherwise the batter is likely to spill, lava-like, right over the edges.

Line the mug with clingfilm if you are planning on turning it out. Alternatively, grease it with a little oil or butter.

COOKING

Place a plate under the mug. This will minimise the clean up should there be an unexpected overflow or explosion!

Be patient. Wait for at least three-quarters of the cooking time before you check on your cake as otherwise it will sink. Don't worry if it does – it will rise again, just follow the directions below. Is it done? If the cake rapidly sinks once you open the microwave door the cake is not cooked through. Return it to the microwave and cook in bursts of 15 seconds until risen and it no longer sinks.

It looks done. If your cake is perfectly risen, touch the top of the sponge in the centre – it should feel firm and slightly springy. You can also try the classic cake test; insert a skewer to the base of the mug and check to see when you remove it that it comes out clean. Alternatively, use a knife to pull the sponge away from the edge to see right to the bottom. If it is still a little uncooked, return to the microwave and cook for short bursts of time taking cake not to over cook. If you'd prefer a slightly gooey centre you might want to leave it a little underdone.

DECORATING

Cool the cake properly before icing to prevent it melting. This could be your desired effect, but not when you go to the effort of beautifully piping your friend's name and it dribbles all over the place.

If you are turning out onto a plate, the cake should come out cleanly as long as you remembered to grease the mug or line it with clingfilm. If you forgot this step, run a small knife or palette knife between the sponge and the mug and ease it out carefully.

ENJOY

Eat straightaway! Mug cakes are best eaten on the day they are made as they dry out more quickly than conventionally baked cakes. If you do want to keep until the next day, either cover with icing to seal in the moisture or wrap well with foil.

GO!

Once you have mastered these points then just have fun – change flavours and toppings to create your own perfect cup of cake!

Classics

CHOCOLATE & PEANUT BUTTER

||||||||||||||||||||||||||||||||||||||||||||||||||||||||||||||||||||||||||||||||||||||||||||||||||||||||||||||||

If you had to work late, your train was delayed or you got caught in the rain...
this is the cake to treat yourself with – it will banish your blues away.

INGREDIENTS

2 tablespoons soft butter

40g dark chocolate, finely chopped

1 medium egg

2 tablespoons semi-skimmed milk

3 tablespoons caster sugar

3 tablespoons self-raising flour

pinch of salt

2 tablespoons smooth peanut butter

1 tablespoon salted roasted peanuts, roughly chopped

METHOD

Place the butter and chocolate in a 350ml mug and microwave for 10–20 seconds until melted.

Add the egg and milk to the mug and beat with a fork until thoroughly combined.

Add the sugar, flour and salt and beat again until smooth, then float a tablespoon of peanut butter on top of the cake mixture but don't stir – this will sink down as the cake cooks to create a lovely gooey peanut butter centre.

Cook in the microwave for 2 minutes 20 seconds @ 600W, 2 minutes @ 800W or 1 minute 40 seconds @ 1000W.

While the cake is still warm, top with the remaining peanut butter. Wait for it to melt slightly and then scatter with peanuts, curl up on the sofa and enjoy.

||||||||||||||||||||||||||||||||||||||||||||||||||||||||||||||||||

Overdose on chocolate –
swap the peanut butter
for chocolate spread.

||||||||||||||||||||||||||||||||||||||||||||||||||||||||||||||||||

CARROT CAKE

Carrot cake as it should be, with pecans, raisins and a delicious cream cheese topping.

INGREDIENTS

2 tablespoons vegetable oil

1 medium egg

1 tablespoon semi-skimmed milk

1 teaspoon vanilla extract

3 tablespoons light brown sugar

4 tablespoons self-raising flour

pinch of salt

$\frac{1}{4}$ teaspoon ground mixed spice

$\frac{1}{4}$ teaspoon ground cinnamon

2 tablespoons grated carrot

$\frac{1}{2}$ tablespoon pecans, roughly chopped

$\frac{1}{2}$ tablespoon raisins

To decorate

2 tablespoons cream cheese

1 tablespoon icing sugar

1 teaspoon lemon juice

$\frac{1}{4}$ teaspoon ground cinnamon

1–2 edible sugar carrots

METHOD

Place the oil, egg, milk, vanilla and sugar in a 350ml mug and beat with a fork until well combined.

Add the flour, salt, mixed spice and cinnamon and beat again until smooth, then fold through the carrot, pecans and raisins. Cook in the microwave for 2 minutes 50 seconds @ 600W, 2 minutes 30 seconds @ 800W or 2 minutes 10 seconds @ 1000W. Leave to cool.

Meanwhile, make the frosting. Beat together the cream cheese, icing sugar and lemon juice until light and fluffy.

Roughly spoon the icing over the cooled sponge. Sprinkle over the cinnamon and top with a sugar carrot or two.

Tip

You can easily make your own carrot toppers with a little marzipan and food colouring.

VANILLA CONES

The perfect tea-time treat for a sunny afternoon! They go down great with kids, so why not trailblaze a trend and serve at parties instead of cupcakes?

INGREDIENTS

2 tablespoons soft butter

1 medium egg

1 tablespoon semi-skimmed milk

2 teaspoons vanilla extract

3 tablespoons caster sugar

4 tablespoons self-raising flour

pinch of salt

4 small flat-bottomed wafer ice cream cones, optional

To decorate

4 tablespoons softened butter

6 tablespoons icing sugar

$^{1}/_{4}$ teaspoon vanilla extract

2 chocolate flakes, halved

1 tablespoon strawberry sauce

1 teaspoon coloured sprinkles

Tip

Alter the icing flavour by adding 1 tablespoon cooled melted chocolate or jam, or 1 teaspoon flavoured essence.

METHOD

Place the butter in a mug and microwave for 10–20 seconds until melted.

Add the egg, milk and vanilla to the mug and beat together with a fork. Add the sugar, flour and salt and beat again until smooth.

Divide between the four ice cream cones and place on a small plate. Cook in the microwave for 1 minute 45 seconds @ 600W, 1 minute 30 seconds @ 800W or 1 minute 15 seconds @ 1000W. Leave to cool.

Meanwhile, make the icing. Beat the butter, icing sugar and vanilla together until light and fluffy, then spoon into a piping bag fitted with a large open star nozzle.

Pipe the icing over the cooled sponge in a spiral pattern – it's best to work from the outside edge, keeping a constant pressure on the icing bag as you work in towards the centre. To finish, release the pressure on the bag, then press down lightly and pull straight up. Decorate with the chocolate flakes and all the sauces and sprinkles you fancy.

If using a 350ml mug, cook in the microwave for 2 minutes 50 seconds @ 600W, 2 minutes 30 seconds @ 800W or 2 minutes 10 seconds @ 1000W. Leave to cool. To make the icing use half the butter, icing sugar and vanilla.

GINGERBREAD

|||||||||||||||||||||||||||||||||||||||||||||||||||||||||||||||||||||||||||||||||||||||||||||||||||||||||||||||

This moist, dark gingerbread is the king of winter warming cakes. When it's cold outside, you can't beat a bit of fiery, toe-tingling spice!

INGREDIENTS

2 tablespoons soft butter

3 tablespoons golden syrup

1 teaspoon black treacle

1 medium egg

3 tablespoons dark soft brown sugar

3 tablespoons self-raising flour

$1/4$ teaspoon ground ginger

$1/4$ teaspoon ground nutmeg

pinch of salt

To decorate

2 tablespoons softened butter

4 tablespoons icing sugar

$1/4$ teaspoon ground cinnamon

1 tablespoon crystallised ginger, sliced

METHOD

Place the butter in a 350ml mug and microwave for 10–20 seconds until melted.

Add the golden syrup, treacle and egg and beat together with a fork. Add the sugar, flour, ginger, nutmeg and salt and beat again until thoroughly combined.

Cook in the microwave for 2 minutes 20 seconds @ 600W, 2 minutes @ 800W or 1 minute 40 seconds @ 1000W. Leave to cool.

Meanwhile, make the icing. Beat the butter, icing sugar and cinnamon together until light and fluffy. Spread the icing over the cooled sponge, swirling with the back of a spoon, and top with the crystallised ginger.

TRIPLE CHOCOLATE CAKE

So decadent but so good! I can't imagine life without chocolate cake, so go on, treat yourself.

INGREDIENTS

2 tablespoons soft butter, plus a little more for greasing
40g dark chocolate, finely chopped
1 medium egg
2 tablespoons semi-skimmed milk
3 tablespoons caster sugar
3 tablespoons self-raising flour
pinch of salt

Chocolate ganache
6 tablespoons double cream
50g dark chocolate, finely chopped

METHOD

First make the chocolate ganache. Place 4 tablespoons of the double cream in a mug and microwave for 30 seconds until nearly boiling. Add the finely chopped chocolate and mix until melted and smooth, then set aside to cool and thicken.

Grease a 350ml mug with a little butter and set aside. Place the remaining butter and chocolate in a second mug and microwave for 10–20 seconds until melted.

Add the egg and milk to the mug and beat with a fork until thoroughly combined. Add the sugar, flour and salt and beat again until smooth.

Tip the cake mixture into the greased mug and cook in the microwave for 2 minutes 20 seconds @ 600W, 2 minutes @ 800W or 1 minute 40 seconds @ 1000W. Leave to cool slightly as the cake will shrink a little from the sides of the mug.

Turn the cake out onto a plate and pour over the ganache to serve. Whip the remaining cream into soft peaks and spoon a flourish on top.

Tip

The longer you leave the ganache, the more it will set, so keep an eye on it.

CHOCOLATE BROWNIE

|||||||||||||||||||||||||||||||||||||||||||||||||||||||||||||||||||||||||||||||||||||||||||||||||||||||||||||||||||||

Make a brownie in a small paper cup or ice cream tub and that way you can slip one into a lunch box or pack up a batch for a picnic.

INGREDIENTS

2 tablespoons soft butter

2 tablespoons caster sugar

1 tablespoon light soft brown sugar

1 tablespoon cocoa powder

1 medium egg yolk

$\frac{1}{2}$ teaspoon vanilla extract

4 tablespoons self-raising flour

pinch of salt

2 tablespoons chocolate chips

METHOD

Place the butter in a 250ml tea cup or small mug and microwave for 10–20 seconds until melted.

Add the caster sugar, brown sugar and cocoa powder and beat with a fork until thoroughly combined.

Add the egg yolk and vanilla and beat together, then add the flour and salt and beat again until thoroughly combined and smooth. Stir through half the chocolate chips and transfer to a 250ml paper cup, if using.

Cook in the microwave for 50 seconds @ 600W, 30 seconds @ 800W or 25 seconds @ 1000W. Scatter the remaining chocolate chips over the top and cook in the microwave for a further 30 seconds. Leave to cool – I recommend for about 15 minutes (if you can bear to wait) as then the cake becomes deliciously chewy and is ready to serve.

Tip Try under-cooking this brownie just a little for a gooey centre… yum!

BANANA BREAD

Moist, sticky and sweet… just the way banana bread should be.

INGREDIENTS

1 medium ripe banana (approx 100g)

1 tablespoon vegetable oil

1 medium egg

1 tablespoon semi-skimmed milk

4 tablespoons light muscovado sugar

4 tablespoons self-raising flour

pinch of salt

¼ teaspoon ground cinnamon

1 tablespoon pecans, roughly chopped

1 tablespoon sultanas

To decorate

2 tablespoons cream cheese

1 tablespoon icing sugar

1 teaspoon lemon juice

¼ teaspoon ground cinnamon

METHOD

In a 350ml mug, mash ¾ of the banana (reserving the rest) with a fork and then beat in the oil, egg and milk until well combined.

Add the sugar, flour, salt and cinnamon and beat again until smooth. Fold through the pecans and sultanas.

Cook in the microwave for 3 minutes 20 seconds @ 600W, 3 minutes @ 800W or 2 minutes 40 seconds @ 1000W. Leave to cool.

Meanwhile, make the frosting. Place the cream cheese, icing sugar and lemon juice in a medium bowl and beat with a fork or a whisk until light and fluffy. Slice the remaining ¼ banana. Spoon the frosting into a piping bag fitted with a closed star nozzle. Pipe at a 45° angle, then top with slices of banana and a dusting of cinnamon. Serve immediately.

Tip Perfect for the sad looking black banana in your fruit bowl.

COFFEE & WALNUT

||||||||||||||||||||||||||||||||||||||||||||||||||||||||||||||||||||||||||||||||||||||||||||||||||||||||||||||||||

*This is an old classic that never goes out of style and in my opinion is the perfect cake for a
mid-morning snack or afternoon tea... especially when it comes with a creamy caramel topping!*

INGREDIENTS

2 tablespoons soft butter

2 teaspoons instant coffee granules
mixed with 1 tablespoon hot water

1 medium egg

1 teaspoon vanilla extract

3 tablespoons golden caster sugar

4 tablespoons self-raising flour

pinch of salt

1 tablespoon walnuts, roughly
chopped

To decorate

2 tablespoons double cream

$^{1}/_{2}$ tablespoon caramel sauce

1 walnut half

METHOD

Place the butter in a 350ml mug and microwave for 10–20
seconds until melted.

Add the coffee, egg, vanilla and sugar to the mug and beat
with a fork until thoroughly combined. Add the flour and salt
and beat again until smooth, then fold through the walnut
pieces. Cook in the microwave for 2 minutes @ 600W,
1 minute 45 seconds @ 800W or 1 minute 30 seconds @
1000W. Leave to cool.

Meanwhile, make the icing. Whip the cream into soft peaks,
fold though the caramel sauce and then spoon over the cooled
sponge and top with the walnut half.

Tip For a little
extra luxury,
replace the double
cream in the icing
with mascarpone.

BLUEBERRY MUFFIN

*This is so delicious and so easy…
just maybe don't get into the habit of eating one for breakfast everyday!*

INGREDIENTS

2 tablespoons soft butter

1 medium egg

1 tablespoon semi-skimmed milk

1 teaspoon vanilla extract

3 tablespoons light brown sugar

4 tablespoons self-raising flour

$\frac{1}{4}$ teaspoon ground cinnamon

pinch of salt

3 tablespoons fresh blueberries

$\frac{1}{2}$ teaspoon demerara sugar

METHOD

Place the butter in a 350ml mug and microwave for 10–20 seconds until melted.

Add the egg, milk and vanilla to the mug and beat with a fork until thoroughly combined.

Add the sugar, flour, cinnamon and salt and beat again until smooth. Fold through half the blueberries and then top with the remainder.

Cook in the microwave for 2 minutes 20 seconds @ 600W, 2 minutes @ 800W or 1 minute 40 seconds @ 1000W.

Sprinkle over the demerara sugar and serve while it is still a little warm.

Swap raspberries for the blueberries or little chunks of pear – and if you do that, throw in a few chocolate chips, too, given they go so well together!

GLUTEN-FREE CHOCOLATE CAKE

Gluten-free flour is widely available and can be used to make very successful mug cakes... so you can have your cake and eat it too!

INGREDIENTS

2 tablespoons soft butter

40g dark chocolate, finely chopped

1 medium egg

2 tablespoons semi-skimmed milk

3 tablespoons caster sugar

3 tablespoons gluten-free flour

¼ teaspoon baking powder

pinch of salt

METHOD

Place the butter and chocolate in a 350ml mug and microwave for 10–20 seconds until melted.

Add the egg and milk to the mug and beat with a fork until thoroughly combined. Add the sugar, flour, baking powder and salt and beat again until smooth.

Cook in the microwave for 2 minutes 20 seconds @ 600W, 2 minutes @ 800W or 1 minute 40 seconds @ 1000W. Leave to cool slightly and serve.

Tip

Feel free to mix and match this sponge with any of the toppings from the book!

EGG-FREE CHOCOLATE CAKE

||||||||||||||||||||||||||||||||||||||||||||||||||||||||||||||||||||||||||||||||||||||||||||||||||||||||||||||||||||||||||

Just because you can't eat egg doesn't mean you can't join in on all the mug cake fun. This eggless cake is just as light, spongy and delicious as its eggy companion.

INGREDIENTS

2 tablespoons soft butter

1 tablespoon cocoa powder

2 tablespoons semi-skimmed milk

1 teaspoon vanilla extract

3 tablespoons light soft brown sugar

4 tablespoons self-raising flour

pinch of salt

2 tablespoons chocolate chips

METHOD

Place the butter in a 300ml mug and microwave for 10–20 seconds until melted.

Add the cocoa powder and beat with a fork until combined. Add the milk, vanilla and sugar to the mug and beat again until smooth.

Add the flour, salt and half the chocolate chips and stir until combined. Scatter the remaining chocolate chips on top.

Cook in the microwave for 1 minute 45 seconds @ 600W, 1 minute 30 seconds @ 800W or 1 minute 15 seconds @ 1000W. Leave to cool.

Tip

Alter the flavour by using other extracts and pick a delicious topping from any of the other mug cakes that take your fancy.

Occasions

BLACK FOREST CAKE

||||||||||||||||||||||||||||||||||||||||||||||||||||||||||||||||||||||||||||||||||||||||||||||||||||||||||||||||||||||||||||||||||||||||||||

Warm, gooey chocolate cake, sweet sticky jam, fresh whipped cream,
rich chocolate curls and a cherry on top… who could want for more?

INGREDIENTS

2 tablespoons soft butter
40g dark chocolate, broken into
small pieces
1 medium egg, lightly beaten
2 tablespoons semi-skimmed milk
3 tablespoons caster sugar
3 tablespoons self-raising flour
pinch of salt
1 tablespoon cherry conserve

To decorate
50ml double cream
1 tablespoon cherry conserve
10g dark chocolate
fresh cherry to garnish

METHOD

Place the butter and chocolate in a 350ml mug and microwave
for 10–20 seconds until melted.

Add the egg and milk to the mug and beat with a fork until
combined.

Add the sugar, flour and salt and beat again until smooth, then
fold through the conserve.

Cook for 2 minutes @ 600W, 1 minute 45 seconds @ 800W or
1 minute 30 seconds @ 1000W. Leave to cool.

Meanwhile, make the icing. Lightly whip the cream into soft
peaks. Spread the conserve over the cooled cake and then
spoon on the whipped cream. Using a vegetable peeler, create
delicate chocolate curls and scatter these over the cream.

Finish, of course, with a cherry on top and serve immediately.

Tip

||||||||||||||||||||||||||||||||||||||||||||||||||||||||

You can serve this cake
warm – just watch out for
dribbling cream!

BIRTHDAY BONANZA

||||||||||||||||||||||||||||||||||||||||||||||||||||||||||||||||||||||||||||||||||||||||||||||||||||||||||||||||||||||||||||||||||

This makes the perfect ready-in-minutes birthday present, plus who would guess it was made in a mug when you dress it up with such fancy icing!

INGREDIENTS

2 tablespoons soft butter
1 medium egg
1 tablespoon semi-skimmed milk
2 teaspoons vanilla extract
3 tablespoons caster sugar
4 tablespoons self-raising flour
pinch of salt
1 tablespoon coloured sprinkles

To decorate
1 teaspoon icing sugar
50g pink ready-to-roll icing
1 tablespoon raspberry jam
3 tablespoons royal icing
1 teaspoon coloured sprinkles
candles

The sponge for
chocolate (see
recipe on page 50).

METHOD

Place the butter in a mug and microwave for 10–20 seconds until melted.

Add the egg, milk and vanilla to the mug and beat with a fork until combined. Add the sugar, flour and salt and beat again until smooth.

Grease or line a 350ml mug with clingfilm, then pour in the cake batter and fold through the coloured sprinkles.

Cook in the microwave for 2 minutes @ 600W, 1 minute 45 seconds @ 800W or 1 minute 30 seconds @ 1000W. Turn the cake out onto a plate, remove the clingfilm and leave to cool.

Meanwhile, prepare the icing. Dust the work surface with the icing sugar and then roll out the pink icing to a size large enough to cover the entire sponge. Spread the jam over the sponge and then lay over the icing, smoothing down with the palm of your hand as you go and trimming offf any excess around the bottom with a sharp knife.

Mix the royal icing with ½ teaspoon water to make an icing the consistency of thick custard. Spoon this icing over the centre of the cake, allowing it to trickle down the sides before it sets. Decorate with coloured sprinkles.

STRAWBERRIES & CREAM VICTORIA SPONGE

||||||||||||||||||||||||||||||||||||||||||||||||||||||||||||||||||||||||||||||||||||||||||||||||||||||||||||||||

This one is a classic English tea-time treat and is really a little too pretty to eat...
but I imagine you will somehow find a way!

INGREDIENTS

2 tablespoons soft butter
1 medium egg
2 tablespoons semi-skimmed milk
1 teaspoon vanilla extract
3 tablespoons caster sugar
4 tablespoons self-raising flour
pinch of salt

To decorate

40ml double cream
1 tablespoon icing sugar
1 tablespoon strawberry jam
1 strawberry, sliced

||||||||||||||||||||||||||||||||||||||||||||||||||

Stir a little elderflower
cordial though the cream
and top with raspberries
for another unbeatable
classic combo.

METHOD

Place the butter in a 350ml mug and microwave for 10–20 seconds until melted.

Add the egg, milk and vanilla to the mug and beat in with a fork until combined. Add the sugar, flour and salt and beat again until smooth.

Cook in the microwave for 1 minute 25 seconds @ 600W, 1 minute 15 seconds @ 800W or 1 minute 5 seconds @ 1000W. Leave to cool.

Meanwhile, make the icing. Using a whisk or a fork, whip the cream and icing sugar into soft peaks.

Spoon the jam over the cake, then add a spoonful of cream. Top with the strawberry and serve with a pot of Earl Grey tea.

ALMOND & BERRY BREAKFAST MUG

Earn yourself a few brownie points by treating your other half to breakfast in bed with this nut and fruit sensation.

INGREDIENTS

2 tablespoons soft butter

1 medium egg

1 tablespoon runny honey

3 tablespoons golden caster sugar

3 tablespoons ground almonds

$\frac{1}{2}$ teaspoon ground cinnamon

3 tablespoons self-raising flour

pinch of salt

3 tablespoons mixed berries

(eg blueberries, raspberries & blackberries)

Streusel topping

2 teaspoons cold butter, finely chopped

$\frac{1}{2}$ tablespoon self-raising flour

$\frac{1}{2}$ tablespoon golden caster sugar

1 teaspoon rolled oats

pinch of ground cinnamon

$\frac{1}{2}$ tablespoon almonds, roughly chopped

METHOD

Place the butter in a 350ml mug and microwave for 10–20 seconds until melted.

Add the egg, honey and sugar to the mug and beat with a fork until combined.

Add the ground almonds, cinnamon, flour and salt and beat again until smooth. Fold through half the berries and then top with the remainder.

To make the streusel, place all the ingredients in a small bowl and rub together with the tips of your fingers to bring together a bit like breadcrumbs.

Spoon the streusel topping over the cake and cook in the microwave for 2 minutes 50 seconds @ 600W, 2 minutes 30 seconds @ 800W or 2 minutes 10 seconds @ 1000W. Leave to cool slightly, then serve.

Tip

This is just as delicious without the streusel toppin so leave it out if you are running late! Or substitut frozen berries. Just defrost slightly before using.

LEMON & POPPY SEED DRIZZLE

Make this cake for your grandma and she will be telling her friends about you and your baking skills for the rest of the year.

INGREDIENTS

2 tablespoons soft butter
1 medium egg
1 tablespoon lemon juice
$\frac{1}{2}$ teaspoon lemon extract
3 tablespoons caster sugar
4 tablespoons self-raising flour
1 teaspoon poppy seeds
pinch of salt

To decorate

3 tablespoons icing sugar
$\frac{1}{4}$ teaspoon lemon extract
pinch of lemon zest

Swap the lemons
for oranges
or use both.

METHOD

Place the butter in a mug and microwave for 10–20 seconds until melted.

Add the egg, lemon juice and lemon extract to the mug and beat with a fork until combined. Add the sugar, flour, poppy seeds and salt and beat again until smooth.

Grease or line a 350ml mug with clingfilm, then pour in the cake batter.

Cook in the microwave for 2 minutes @ 600W, 1 minute 45 seconds @ 800W or 1 minute 30 seconds @ 1000W. Turn the cake out onto a plate, remove the clingfilm and leave to cool.

Meanwhile, make the icing. Mix together the icing sugar and lemon extract, adding a drop of water to thin it if necessary. Spoon the icing over the cake so that it trickles down the sides before it sets, then top with the lemon zest and serve.

BRAMBLE CAKE

||||||||||||||||||||||||||||||||||||||||||||||||||||||||||||||||||||||||||||||||||||||||||||||||||||||||||||||

The humble blackberry, teamed with almond, is a force to be reckoned with. So raid the hedgerows when they're nice, plump and juicy and stock up the freezer.

INGREDIENTS

2 tablespoons soft butter

1 medium egg

1 tablespoon semi-skimmed milk

1 teaspoon almond extract

3 tablespoons light brown sugar

3 tablespoons ground almonds

3 tablespoons self-raising flour

pinch of salt

15g marzipan, diced

50g fresh blackberries

To decorate

½ teaspoon demerara sugar

½ tablespoon flaked almonds

METHOD

Place the butter in a 350ml mug and microwave for 10–20 seconds until melted.

Add the egg, milk, almond extract and sugar to the mug and beat with a fork until combined. Add the ground almonds, flour and salt and beat again until smooth. Fold through the marzipan and half the blackberries, then top with the remainder.

Cook in the microwave for 3 minutes 35 seconds @ 600W, 3 minutes 15 seconds @ 800W or 2 minute 55 seconds @ 1000W. Leave to cool.

Sprinkle over the demerara sugar and flaked almonds and serve.

Tip This is also delicious with the addition of 1 tablespoon grated apple.

HONEY CAKE

A little extra effort goes into this one, but when your best friend sees those little buzzy bees, you'll know it was all worth it.

INGREDIENTS

2 tablespoons soft butter

1 medium egg

2 tablespoons runny honey

$^1/_2$ teaspoon vanilla extract

3 tablespoons light muscavado sugar

4 tablespoons self-raising flour

pinch of salt

To decorate

2 tablespoons softened butter

4 tablespoons icing sugar

pinch of ground cinnamon

30g yellow marzipan

black food dye

4 flaked almonds

cocktail stick

1 teaspoon honey

Tip

Making the marzipan bees a day in advance means they will firm up a little and hold their shape.

METHOD

Place the butter in a 350ml mug and microwave for 10–20 seconds until melted.

Add the egg, honey and vanilla to the mug and beat with a fork until combined. Add the sugar, flour and salt and beat again until smooth.

Cook in the microwave for 1 minute 45 seconds @ 600W, 1 minute 30 seconds @ 800W or 1 minute 15 seconds @ 1000W. Leave to cool.

Meanwhile, make the icing. Beat the butter, icing sugar and cinnamon together until light and fluffy, then spoon into a piping bag fitted with a large round nozzle.

Divide the marzipan in two and, with your fingers, roll each piece into two bumble bee-sized oval shapes. Dipping either a skewer or a paintbrush into the black food dye, paint the marzipan with stripes and eyes to look like a bee, finishing with almond flakes for wings. Place one on a cocktail stick.

Once the cake is completely cooled, pipe the icing in a spiral pattern over the sponge. It's best to work from the outside edge inward and to keep constant pressure on the icing bag. To finish, release the pressure on the bag, press down lightly and then pull straight up.

Garnish with the bees and drizzle with honey to serve.

RAINBOW CAKE

This colourful cake is the perfect pick-me-up so make it for anyone you notice is looking a little down. The rainclouds will clear and the sun will come out.

INGREDIENTS

2 tablespoons soft butter
1 medium egg
1 tablespoon semi-skimmed milk
1 teaspoon vanilla extract
3 tablespoons caster sugar
4 tablespoons self-raising flour
pinch of salt
pink, yellow, green and blue food colouring

To decorate
1 tablespoon soft butter
2 tablespoons icing sugar
¼ teaspoon vanilla extract
1 rainbow marshmallow twist

Tip

Add the food colouring a little at a time as too much can ruin the taste. If using colouring pastes, use the end of a cocktail stick to scoop out a little at a time.

METHOD

Place the butter in a 350ml mug and microwave for 10–20 seconds until melted.

Add the egg, milk and vanilla to the mug and beat with a fork until combined. Add the sugar, flour and salt and beat again until smooth.

Divide the cake mixture between 4 small pots. Add a few drops of different food colouring to each pot and mix in well.

Spoon each of the coloured cake mixtures into a 350ml mug and use a skewer or knife to swirl together the colours for a beautiful marble effect.

Cook in the microwave for 2 minutes @ 600W, 1 minute 45 seconds @ 800W or 1 minute 30 seconds @ 1000W. Leave to cool.

Meanwhile, make the icing. Beat the butter, icing sugar and vanilla together until light and fluffy, then spoon into a piping bag fitted with a closed star nozzle. Pipe two 2–3cm whirls.

Take a marshmallow twist, bend it and stick each end into the icing to create a lovely rainbow arch, then serve.

HALLOWEEN GHOST

This is so simple to make and decorate, it guarantees ghoulish fun for all ages.

INGREDIENTS

2 tablespoons soft butter, plus a little for greasing

40g dark chocolate

1 medium egg

2 tablespoons semi-skimmed milk

3 tablespoons caster sugar

3 tablespoons self-raising flour

pinch of salt

For the chocolate ganache

4 tablespoons double cream

60g dark chocolate, finely chopped

To decorate

1 teaspoon icing sugar

75–100g white ready-to-roll icing

black food colouring

Swap the sponge for vanilla (see recipe on page 38) and spread with either the ganache or jam.

METHOD

First make the chocolate ganache. Place the cream in a mug and microwave for 20–30 seconds until nearly boiling. Add the chocolate and stir until melted and smooth. Set aside to cool a little and thicken. The longer you leave the ganache, the more it will set so keep an eye on it to make sure you get a nice and thick but spreadable icing.

Grease a 350ml mug with a little butter and set aside. Place the remaining butter and chocolate into a second mug and microwave for 10–20 seconds until melted.

Add the egg and milk to the mug and beat together with a fork, then add the sugar, flour and salt and beat again until smooth. Transfer the cake mixture to the greased mug and cook in the microwave for 2 minutes 20 seconds @ 600W, 2 minutes @ 800W or 1 minute 40 seconds @ 1000W. Turn the cake out onto a plate and leave to cool slightly.

Spread the ganache over the cooled sponge. Dust a clean work surface with the icing sugar and roll out the icing to a size that will cover the entire cake. Cut a rough 16cm round circle out of the icing and gently lay this over the ganache-covered sponge. Press down a little on top but leave the edges to fold slightly in waves.

Dip a paintbrush or cocktail stick in the black food colouring and draw on a face.

RED VELVET CAKE

||||||||||||||||||||||||||||||||||||||||||||||||||||||||||||||||||||||||||||||||||||||||||||||||||||||||||||

A card is boring, maybe flowers are too much, but a red velvet cake with cream cheese frosting is just the ticket come Valentine's Day.

INGREDIENTS

2 tablespoons soft butter

1 medium egg

1 teaspoon red food colouring

2 tablespoons buttermilk

1 teaspoon vanilla extract

3 tablespoons caster sugar

3 tablespoons self-raising flour

1$\frac{1}{2}$ tablespoons cocoa powder

pinch of salt

$\frac{1}{4}$ teaspoon white wine vinegar

To decorate

1 tablespoon soft butter

1$\frac{1}{2}$ tablespoons cream cheese

3 tablespoons icing sugar

$\frac{1}{4}$ teaspoon red food colouring

METHOD

Place the butter in a 350ml mug and microwave for 10–20 seconds until melted.

Add the egg, red food colouring, buttermilk and vanilla to the mug and beat with a fork until combined.

Add the sugar, flour, cocoa and salt and beat again until smooth. Stir in the white wine vinegar.

Cook in the microwave for 2 minutes @ 600W, 1 minute 45 seconds @ 800W or 1 minute 30 seconds @ 1000W. Leave to cool.

Meanwhile, make the icing. Beat the butter, cream cheese and icing sugar together until smooth. Add the red food colouring one drop at a time, stirring after each addition until you achieve your desired shade of red, then spoon the icing into a piping bag fitted with a closed star nozzle.

The effect you want from your icing is that of a beautiful Valentine's rose so start in the centre and, keeping steady pressure on the piping bag, move in a gradual spiral towards the outer edge, overlapping a little as you go. To finish, release pressure on the piping bag, press down slightly and then pull away.

CHRISTMAS CAKE

||||||||||||||||||||||||||||||||||||||||||||||||||||||||||||||||||||||||||||||||||||||||||||||||||||||||||||||

*Everyone loves a Christmas cake for the holidays and the added appeal of this one is
that you can make it in no time at all and without all the advance planning... genius!*

INGREDIENTS

1 tablespoon soft butter, plus a little
for greasing

1 tablespoon brandy

6 tablespoons mixed dried fruit

1 medium egg

3 tablespoons dark brown sugar

$1/2$ teaspoon mixed spice

$1/2$ teaspoon ground cinnamon

1 teaspoon vanilla extract

1 tablespoon self-raising flour

pinch of salt

1 tablespoon glacé cherries, halved

1 tablespoon candied peel

2 tablespoons almonds, roughly
chopped

To decorate

1 teaspoon icing sugar

75g ready-to-roll marzipan

1 tablespoon apricot jam

75g ready-to-roll icing

3 tablespoons royal icing

$1/2$ teaspoon water

$1/2$ teaspoon white sprinkles

$1/4$ teaspoon edible gold stars

METHOD

Grease a 350ml mug with a little butter and set aside. Place
the butter, brandy and dried fruit in a mug and microwave for
10–20 seconds until melted. Add the egg, sugar, mixed spice,
cinnamon and vanilla and beat with a fork until combined.
Add the flour, salt, glacé cherries, candied peel and almonds
and fold through.

Cook in the microwave for 3 minutes 20 seconds @ 600W,
3 minutes @ 800W or 2 minutes 40 seconds @ 1000W. Leave
to cool until it comes away from the edges then turn out onto
a plate to cool completely.

Dust a clean work surface with the icing sugar and roll out
the marzipan to a size large enough to cover the entire cake.
Brush the cake with half the jam then lay over the marzipan,
smoothing it down with your palm as you go, trimming any
excess at the bottom with a sharp knife. Repeat the process
with the ready-to-roll icing.

Mix the royal icing with the water to a thick consistency. Spoon
over the centre of the iced cake and allow to dribble down the
sides. While still wet, scatter over the sprinkles and gold stars.

Tip

||||||||||||||||||||||||||||||||||||||||||||||||||||||||||||||||||||||||||||||||||

Wrap in baking parchment and
then coloured tissue for a perfect
homemade foodie gift.

||||||||||||||||||||||||||||||||||||||||||||||||||||||||||||||||||||||||||||||||||

Happy Hour

PINA COLADA

This cake guarantees a little ray of sunshine on a cold winter's day.
Set up the deckchair, break out the cocktail umbrellas and enjoy!

INGREDIENTS

$^1/_2$ tablespoon desiccated coconut

1 medium egg, yolk and white
separated

50g fresh pineapple, finely chopped,
plus a slice for garnish

2 tablespoons soft butter

1 tablespoon white rum

3 tablespoons caster sugar

2 tablespoons coconut milk

1 teaspoon vanilla extract

5 tablespoons self-raising flour

pinch of salt

To garnish

2 tablespoons double cream

$^1/_2$ tablespoon icing sugar

1 tablespoon rum

1 small pineapple slice and 1 leaf

1 glacé cherry

$^1/_2$ tablespoon coconut flakes

1 cocktail umbrella

METHOD

Tip the desiccated coconut onto a small plate and spread out to cover. Take a 350ml mug and dip the rim first into the egg white and then into the coconut. Try and stick as much coconut as you can to the edge of the mug.

Add the pineapple, butter, rum and caster sugar to the mug and microwave for 1 minute until hot and bubbling. Leave to cool slightly.

Add the remaining egg white, egg yolk, coconut milk and vanilla to the mug and beat with a fork until thoroughly combined. Add the flour and salt and beat again until smooth.

Cook in the microwave for 5 minutes 30 seconds @ 600W, 4 minutes 30 seconds @ 800W or 3 minutes 30 seconds @ 1000W. Leave to cool.

Meanwhile, make the icing. Beat together the cream, icing sugar and rum until light and fluffy, then spread over the sponge, swirling with the back of a spoon. Garnish with the pineapple slice, pineapple leaf, cherry and coconut, then add a big cocktail umbrella.

Tip

Make this non-alcoholic using pineapple juice in place of rum.

COKE FLOAT

Don't make the kids miss out on the happy hour fun – this old classic is just for them! Oh and of course all the big kids as well.

INGREDIENTS

2 tablespoons soft butter

1 tablespoon cocoa powder

1 medium egg

2 tablespoons cola

3 tablespoons golden caster sugar

4 tablespoons self-raising flour

pinch of salt

To decorate

2 teaspoons soft butter

$\frac{1}{2}$ teaspoon cocoa powder

2 tablespoons icing sugar

1 teaspoon cola

1 scoop vanilla ice cream

1 tablespoon fizzy cola bottles

METHOD

Place the butter in a 350ml mug and microwave for 10–20 seconds until melted.

Add the cocoa and mix until well combined. Add the egg, cola and sugar to the mug and beat together with a fork. Add the flour and salt and beat again until smooth.

Cook in the microwave for 2 minutes 20 seconds @ 600W, 2 minutes @ 800W or 1 minute 40 seconds @ 1000W. Leave to cool.

Meanwhile, make the icing. Place the butter, cocoa powder, icing sugar and cola in a mug and stir together. Cook in the microwave for 10–15 seconds until melted, then stir again until smooth.

Top the cake with a scoop of ice cream and drizzle with the icing. Top with the cola bottles.

Go all out and make
cherry cola floats!
Use cherry cola in
the cake and top with
cherry ice cream.

MOCHA

When you're working late and you need something to keep going, this is just the ticket – well, I'll make any excuse for a bit of cake!

INGREDIENTS

1 tablespoon soft butter

20g dark chocolate, finely chopped

1 medium egg

1 tablespoon semi-skimmed milk

2 teaspoons instant coffee granules, mixed with 1$\frac{1}{2}$ tablespoons hot water

2 tablespoons light brown soft sugar

2 tablespoons self-raising flour

pinch of salt

To decorate

1 tablespoon extra thick double cream

pinch of cocoa powder

1 teaspoon coffee beans

METHOD

Place the butter and chocolate in a small 200ml mug or teacup and microwave for 10–20 seconds until melted.

Add the egg, milk and half the coffee to the mug and beat with a fork until thoroughly combined. Add the sugar, flour and salt and beat again until smooth.

Cook in the microwave for 2 minutes @ 600W, 1 minute 45 seconds @ 800W or 1 minute 30 seconds @ 1000W.

Pierce the cake numerous times with a cocktail stick and pour over the remaining coffee, then leave to cool slightly.

Top the cake with a thick swirl of cream, a dusting of cocoa and one or two coffee beans.

Tip

Pouring the coffee over the cake keeps it moist and gives it a more intense coffee flavour than mixing it all in with the batter.

BAILEYS ON THE ROCKS

This one's a smooth-flavoured Irish cream cake for grown ups with a few marshmallows for those days when you need extra indulgence.

INGREDIENTS

2 tablespoons soft butter
¹/₂ teaspoon cocoa powder
1 medium egg
2 tablespoons Baileys or other Irish cream liqueur
3 tablespoons golden caster sugar
3 tablespoons self-raising flour
pinch of salt

To decorate
3 white marshmallows
1 teaspoon Baileys

METHOD

Place the butter in a 350ml mug and microwave for 10–20 seconds until melted.

Add the cocoa to the mug and mix together, then add the egg and Baileys and beat with a fork until thoroughly combined. Finally add the sugar, flour and salt and beat again until smooth.

Cook in the microwave for 2 minutes @ 600W, 1 minute 45 seconds @ 800W or 1 minute 30 seconds @ 1000W.

Top with the marshmallows and microwave for a further 10–15 seconds until just melting. Drizzle over the Baileys and serve.

Tip

Why not try this topping on a brownie, a chocolate cake or even melt it completely and drizzle over a sundae!

GUINNESS CAKE

||||||||||||||||||||||||||||||||||||||||||||||||||||||||||||||||||||||||||||||||||||||||||||||||||||||

*Dense and moist, this velvety Guinness cake makes a perfect thank you for Dad
when he has agreed to pick you up from that late-night party.*

INGREDIENTS

2 tablespoons soft butter
40g dark chocolate, broken
into pieces
1 medium egg
3 tablespoons Guinness or
other stout
3 tablespoons soft dark brown sugar
4 tablespoons self-raising flour
pinch of salt

To decorate

3 tablespoons icing sugar
1 1/2 tablespoons cream cheese
1/2 tablespoon white sprinkles

METHOD

Place the butter and chocolate in a 350ml mug and microwave
for 10–20 seconds until melted.

Add the egg to the mug and beat with a fork until combined.
Stir though the Guinness, then add the sugar, flour and salt and
beat again until smooth.

Cook in the microwave for 2 minutes @ 600W, 1 minute
45 seconds @ 800W or 1 minute 30 seconds @ 1000W. Leave
to cool.

Meanwhile, make the icing. Beat the icing sugar and cream
cheese together until smooth, then spread over the cooled cake,
swirling with the back of a spoon. Scatter with the sprinkles
to serve.

WHITE RUSSIAN

Make a statement with this amazing monochrome cocktail. The creamy marbled flavours work deliciously together and give this cocktail cake a real twist.

INGREDIENTS

2 tablespoons soft butter

1 medium egg

3 tablespoons caster sugar

4 tablespoons self-raising flour

pinch of salt

1 tablespoon Kahlua or coffee liqueur

1 teaspoon cocoa powder

1 tablespoon vodka

1 teaspoon vanilla extract

To decorate

3 tablespoons double cream

1 tablespoon Kahlua

pinch cocoa powder

black and white striped straws

METHOD

Place the butter in a 350ml mug and microwave for 10–20 seconds until melted.

Add the egg and sugar and beat with a fork until combined, then add the flour and salt and beat again until smooth. Spoon half of the cake mixture into another mug or bowl and stir though the Kahlua and cocoa powder. Stir the vodka and vanilla through the other half.

Combine the two cake mixtures in one 350ml mug but do not mix – simply drag through a skewer or knife to creat a marble effect. Cook in the microwave for 2 minutes 20 seconds @ 600W, 2 minutes @ 800W or 1 minute 40 seconds @ 1000W. Leave to cool.

Meanwhile, make the icing. Whisk the double cream into soft peaks and then stir through the Kahlua. Spoon the icing over the cake and sprinkle with the cocoa powder. Serve with little black and white straws.

 Swap Make this non-alcoholic using coffee or melted chocolate place of Kahlua and milk instead of vodka.

MOJITO

A classic refreshing drink turned into a funky mug cake! This will remind you of your holidays and perhaps tempt you to book another.

INGREDIENTS

2 tablespoons soft butter
1 medium egg
1 tablespoon white rum
4 tablespoons caster sugar
1 lime, zested
1 tablespoon lime juice
3 tablespoons self-raising flour
pinch of salt

To decorate
2 tablespoons soft butter
4 tablespoons icing sugar
$\frac{1}{4}$ teaspoon peppermint essence
drop of green food colouring
1 slice of lime
1 teaspoon caster sugar
3 mini white marshmallows
1 cocktail stick
1 fresh mint sprig

This makes a great dessert and your friends will love the quirky presentation.

METHOD

Place the butter in a 350ml mug and microwave for 10–20 seconds until melted.

Add the egg, rum, sugar, lime zest and juice to the mug and beat with a fork until combined. Add the flour and salt and beat again until smooth.

Cook in the microwave for 1 minute then a further 1 minute 10 seconds @ 600W, 1 minute @ 800W or 50 seconds @ 1000W. Leave to cool.

Meanwhile, make the icing. Beat the butter, icing sugar and peppermint together until light and fluffy, then fold through the green colouring. Spoon into a piping bag fitted with a large closed star nozzle. Pipe the icing over the cooled sponge in a spiral pattern – it's best to work in from the outside edge, keeping constant pressure on the icing bag and working gradually towards the centre. To finish, release the pressure on the bag, then press down lightly and pull straight up.

Dip the lime slice in a little water and then roll the edge through the sugar. Thread the marshmallows onto the cocktail stick and skewer into the top of the cake. Finish with the sugared lime and a mint sprig.

Treats
&
Puds

SALTED CARAMEL & CHOCOLATE

Salted caramel is ridiculously addictive. Here the salt sets off the caramel and dark chocolate perfectly.

INGREDIENTS

2 tablespoons soft butter, plus a little for greasing

40g dark chocolate, finely chopped

1 medium egg

1 tablespoon semi-skimmed milk

2 tablespoons light brown sugar

3 tablespoons self-raising flour

2 tablespoons dulche de leche or thick caramel, mixed with $\frac{1}{4}$ teaspoon sea salt flakes

pinch of sea salt flakes

METHOD

Grease a 350ml mug with a little butter.

Place the remaining butter and chocolate in a second mug and microwave for 10–20 seconds until melted.

Add the egg and milk and beat with a fork until combined. Add the sugar and flour and beat again until smooth, then transfer the mixture to the greased mug and spoon a tablespoon of the salty caramel on the top.

Cook in the microwave for 3 minutes 20 seconds @ 600W, 3 minutes @ 800W or 2 minutes 40 seconds @ 1000W. Leave to cool.

Carefully turn the cake out onto a plate and spoon over the remaining caramel. Sprinkle with a few sea salt flakes and serve immediately.

Top with a scoop of vanilla, chocolate or caramel ice cream.

LAMINGTONS

A traditional Australian treat and a school fête favourite! These little cakes are as fun and messy to make as they are to eat!

INGREDIENTS

2 tablespoons soft butter, plus a little to grease

1 medium egg

1 tablespoon semi-skimmed milk

2 teaspoons vanilla extract

3 tablespoons caster sugar

4 tablespoons self-raising flour

pinch of salt

To decorate

2 tablespoons butter

1 teaspoon cocoa powder

3 tablespoons icing sugar

3 tablespoons desiccated coconut

3 tablespoons double cream

1 tablespoon strawberry jam

Tip

Purists wouldn't slice the sponge and serve with cream and jam so leave it out if you wish.

METHOD

Grease a 350ml mug with a little butter and set aside.
Place the butter in a second mug and microwave for 10–20 seconds until melted.

Add the egg, milk and vanilla to the mug and beat with a fork until combined. Add the sugar, flour and salt and beat again until smooth.

Cook in the microwave for 2 minutes 20 seconds @ 600W, 2 minutes @ 800W or 1 minute 40 seconds @ 1000W. Leave to cool.

Meanwhile, make the icing. Place the butter, cocoa powder and icing sugar in a mug and microwave for 10–15 seconds until melted. Stir to combine.

Scatter the coconut evenly over a plate. Turn the cooled sponge out of the mug and then dip the entire cake in the chocolate icing. Immediately transfer the chocolate-coated cake to the plate and roll so the coconut is distributed evenly over the surface. Leave for a few minutes while you wait for the icing to set.

Meanwhile, whip the cream into soft peaks. Slice the cake in half horizontally and spread the top of the bottom sponge with the jam. Add a spoon of whipped cream and then top with the other sponge half.

RASPBERRY & PISTACHIO RICE CRISPIES

*Okay, so you might argue that this is not strictly a cake and I would insist
that it is (it's a crispie cake), but whichever side of the fence you land on,
I am sure we will both agree that it's one of the tastiest things that
has ever come out of a microwave.*

INGREDIENTS

4 tablespoons marshmallow fluff
or marshmallows
6 tablespoons Rice Crispies
1 tablespoon dark chocolate chunks
1 tablespoon dried raspberries
1 tablespoon pistachios, roughly
chopped

METHOD

Place the marshmallow fluff in a 350ml mug and microwave
for 10–15 seconds until melted.

Fold through the Rice Crispies, chocolate chunks, raspberries
and pistachios.

Cook in the microwave for 12 seconds @ 600W, 10 seconds
@ 800W or 8 seconds @ 1000W.

Serve warm and gooey or leave to set and enjoy like a crispy
cake.

Tip

If you like your crispy cake to be slightly chewy, line your
mug with clingfilm before you start. Once cooked, turn it
out onto a plate, remove the clingfilm and leave to cool.

CHOCOLATE, GINGER & PEAR CAKE

If you ever need a posh dessert in a hurry — this is it. It's simple to whip up, and sophisticated enough for the classiest soirée.

INGREDIENTS

1 tablespoon soft butter
20g dark chocolate, finely chopped
$^1/_2$ medium egg, lightly beaten
1 tablespoon semi-skimmed milk
2 tablespoons caster sugar
2 tablespoons self-raising flour
$^1/_4$ teaspoon ground ginger
pinch of salt
1 tablespoon stem ginger, finely chopped
1 ripe pear, peeled

To decorate
1 tablespoon stem ginger syrup
pinch of cocoa powder

METHOD

Place the butter and chocolate in a 350ml mug and microwave for 10–20 seconds until melted.

Add the egg and milk to the mug and beat in with a fork until combined.

Add the sugar, flour, ground ginger and salt and beat again until smooth. Fold through the chopped stem ginger.
Slice off the base of the pear so it will sit up in the mug and then press down into the mixture.

Cook in the microwave for 2 minutes 10 seconds @ 600W, 1 minute 50 seconds @ 800W or 1 minute 30 seconds @ 1000W. Leave to cool.

Drizzle with a little stem ginger syrup and dust with cocoa powder, then serve.

Swap
Swap the dark chocolate for white and add $^1/_2$ teaspoon vanilla extract.

CHOCOLATE CHIP COOKIE

||||||||||||||||||||||||||||||||||||||||||||||||||||||||||||||||||||||||||||||||||||||||||||||||||||||||||||||||||||||||||||||||||||||

Once again I have snuck in a recipe that isn't really a cake, but then variety is the spice of life and you'll want this instant cookie recipe in your microwave repertoire... trust me.

INGREDIENTS

1 tablespoon soft butter

1 tablespoon caster sugar

1 tablespoon dark soft brown sugar

1 medium egg yolk

¼ teaspoon vanilla extract

3 tablespoons plain flour

pinch of salt

2 tablespoons chocolate chips

METHOD

Place the butter in a large ramekin or small mug and microwave for 10–20 seconds until melted.

Add the caster sugar, brown sugar and egg yolk and beat together with a fork. Add the vanilla, flour and salt and beat again until combined, then fold through the chocolate chips (leaving a few at the top, which will go gooey). Flatten the dough with the back of a spoon.

Cook in the microwave for 1 minute 10 seconds @ 600W, 1 minute @ 800W or 50 seconds @ 1000W. Leave to stand for 10 minutes.

Tip If you leave this cookie to stand for 10 minutes, it will still be warm but also deliciously chewy.

STICKY TOFFEE

If someone catches you eating this mug of pure bliss and suggests that you might like to share with them, next time be sure to lock the kitchen door.

INGREDIENTS

2 tablespoons soft butter, plus a little for greasing

4 tablespoons toffee sauce

1 medium egg

1 teaspoon vanilla extract

2 tablespoons dried dates, roughly chopped

3 tablespoons dark muscavado sugar

4 tablespoons self-raising flour

pinch of ground cloves

pinch of salt

METHOD

Grease a 350ml mug with a little butter and then spoon in 3 tablespoons of the toffee sauce.

Place the butter in a second mug and microwave for 10–20 seconds until melted.

Add the egg, a tablespoon of toffee sauce, the vanilla and dried dates and beat together with a fork.

Fold in the sugar, flour, ground cloves and salt and beat again until smooth and then spoon this cake mixture into the mug with the toffee sauce.

Cook in the microwave for 2 minutes 35 seconds @ 600W, 2 minutes 15 seconds @ 800W or 1 minute 55 seconds @ 1000W. Leave to cool.

Carefully turn the cake out onto a plate, ensuring you scrape all the toffee goodness from the bottom of the mug and none goes to waste! Serve immediately with a scoop of ice cream if you wish.

Tip

Mix a tablespoon of cocoa powder in with the flour to bring a little chocolate flavour to the party.

ROCKY ROAD

||||||||||||||||||||||||||||||||||||||||||||||||||||||||||||||||||||||||||||||||||||||||||||||||||||||||||||||||||||

Rocky road is the stuff that dreams are made of, so get in the kitchen and make yours come utterly deliciously true!

INGREDIENTS

2 tablespoons soft butter

1 tablespoon cocoa powder

1 medium egg

3 tablespoons caster sugar

2 tablespoons self-raising flour

pinch of salt

4 tablespoons mini marshmallows

2 tablespoons raisins

2 tablespoons plain biscuits broken,

such as digestives

METHOD

Place the butter in a 350ml mug and microwave for 10–20 seconds until melted.

Stir in the cocoa powder until combined, then add the egg and sugar and beat with a fork until combined.

Add the flour and salt and beat again until smooth. Fold through almost all the marshmallows, raisins and biscuits and then top with the remaining.

Cook in the microwave for 2 minutes 20 seconds @ 600W, 2 minutes @ 800W or 1 minute 40 seconds @ 1000W. Leave to cool slightly before tucking in.

Tip

There are so many possible variations with this cake, so have fun adding nuts, using different dried fruit and swapping in different biscuits like chocolate chip cookies.

CHOCOLATE FUDGE S'MORES

S'mores, a traditional American campfire treat, inspired this little mug cake recipe and provided the perfect excuse to eat lots of marshmallows.

INGREDIENTS

2 tablespoons soft butter
2 tablespoons cocoa powder
1 medium egg
2 tablespoons semi-skimmed milk
3 tablespoons caster sugar
3 tablespoons self-raising flour
pinch of salt
30g crushed biscuit (digestives or cookies)
2 tablespoons marshmallow fluff or marshmallows

METHOD

Place the butter in a mug and microwave for 10–20 seconds until melted.

Stir in the cocoa powder until combined, then add the egg and milk and beat with a fork until combined. Add the sugar, flour and salt and beat again until smooth.

Press the crushed biscuit into the bottom of a 350ml mug. Spoon over the cake mixture and carefully top with the marshmallow.

Cook in the microwave for 2 minutes @ 600W, 1 minute 45 seconds @ 800W or 1 minute 30 seconds @ 1000W. Serve immediately.

Tip

As a nod to the classic S'mores, place the mug under the grill for 30 seconds until the marshmallow is nicely caramelised and chewy. Just make sure you use a robust mug!

CHOCOLATE & CARAMEL POPCORN SUNDAE

Make this cake when you're in the mood for a movie night treat. Pile it high with ice cream, popcorn and delicious sweet sauce. Don't forget a saucer to catch the drips!

INGREDIENTS

2 tablespoons soft butter

40g dark chocolate, finely chopped

1 medium egg

2 tablespoons semi-skimmed milk

3 tablespoons caster sugar

3 tablespoons self-raising flour

pinch of salt

To decorate

1 scoop vanilla ice cream

25g toffee popcorn

1 tablespoon caramel sauce

1 tablespoon chocolate sauce

METHOD

Place the butter and chocolate in a 300ml sundae glass and microwave for 10–20 seconds until melted.

Add the egg and milk to the glass and beat with a fork until combined. Add the sugar, flour and salt and beat again until smooth.

Cook in the microwave for 2 minutes 20 seconds @ 600W, 2 minutes @ 800W or 1 minute 40 seconds @ 1000W. Leave to cool slightly.

Top with a scoop of ice cream, scatter with popcorn and finish with a generous drizzle of both sauces.

UPSIDE-DOWN APPLE & CINNAMON CAKE

This sticky upside-down cake can be made with a variety of fruits but here
I marry up a classic pair – apple and cinnamon – with a little caramel sauce.

INGREDIENTS

2 tablespoons soft butter, plus a little for greasing

3 thin slices of red skinned apple

1 medium egg

1 tablespoon semi-skimmed milk

1 teaspoon vanilla extract

3 tablespoons soft brown sugar

4 tablespoons self-raising flour

1 teaspoon ground cinnamon

pinch of salt

3 tablespoons grated apple

To decorate

1 tablespoon caramel sauce

¼ teaspoon demerara sugar

ice cream, optional

METHOD

Grease a 350ml mug with a little butter, then fan out the apple slices and place at the bottom.

Place the remaining butter in a second mug and microwave for 10–20 seconds until melted.

Add the egg, milk and vanilla to the melted butter and beat with a fork until combined.

Add the sugar, flour, cinnamon and salt and beat again until smooth. Fold through the grated apple then gently pour the mixture over the sliced apple.

Cook in the microwave for 2 minutes 20 seconds @ 600W, 2 minutes @ 800W or 1 minute 40 seconds @ 1000W. Leave to cool slightly.

Carefully turn the cake out onto a plate. Drizzle with caramel sauce and scatter with demerara sugar to serve. Add a scoop of ice cream if you like.

LEMON CURD CHEESECAKE

Instant cheesecake... a great invention, but also slightly dangerous! Don't forget to chill this one properly before eating it, as that is when it tastes the best.

INGREDIENTS

$^1/_2$ tablespoon soft butter

30g crushed plain biscuit, such as digestives

1 medium egg

3 tablespoons cream cheese

2 tablespoons soured cream

$^1/_4$ teaspoon vanilla extract

3 tablespoons caster sugar

$^1/_4$ teaspoon cornflour

pinch of salt

To decorate

2 tablespoons lemon curd

1 long piece of curled lemon zest

METHOD

Place the butter in a 300ml jar or mug and microwave for 10–20 seconds until melted. Stir through the biscuit crumbs and then press down with the back of a spoon to create a crust at the bottom of the mug.

In a separate mug add the egg, cream cheese, soured cream, vanilla, caster sugar, cornflour and salt. Beat together with a fork until smooth and combined and then spoon the mixture over the biscuit crust.

Cook in the microwave in 30 second bursts with 20 second breaks in between for 2 minutes @ 600W, 1 minute 45 seconds @ 800W or 1 minute 30 seconds @ 1000W.

Chill in the fridge for at least 1 hour before topping with the lemon curd and lemon zest curl.

Tip

Sometimes it's a good idea to break up the cooking time so that the mixture doesn't overheat and explode! That's the reasoning behind cooking this one in a few short bursts.

INDEX

THANK YOUS

Where to start, what a whirlwind! This book has come together in such a short period. It is incredible what you can accomplish with an amazing team. The recent and instant interest in mug cakes put the wheels in motion at a speed we were not expecting. So thank you to everyone at Kyle Books who helped to shape the book into what you see now. It really was a great team effort.

To Judith and Kyle, thank you for believing in me and giving me the chance to get *Mug Cakes* out there and into people's microwaves! What a fun and exciting subject for my cookbook debut. To Claire, thank you for all your great support behind the scenes.

The lovely Vicki, you made me laugh throughout. Your support and advice was invaluable. I hope your new microwave has you 'mug caking', as well as warming up milk for your new arrival. And once again to Judith, who took over seamlessly; you are always a step ahead and it's a delight to work with you.

Olivia and Wei, thank you both for searching London high and low for the perfect mugs and for all the fun, quirky bits and bobs in between. Nicky, thank you for bringing your wonderful style to *Mug Cakes*. It brings all our hard work together perfectly.

To Tara, who took on the challenge of bringing *Mug Cakes* to life; no one could have more enthusiasm for mugs, cakes and crazy toppings than you. Thank you for being excited about each and every mug cake I put in front of you and your camera.

And finally to Tom, for being utterly disappointed if there wasn't a cake to taste, for your MasterChef-style critiques, your endless support and for 'food styling' my dinner when all I had eaten all day was cake. Your enthusiasm could not have been heightened, even if it was your own book. You are truly wonderful.

THANK YOUS